AGING WELL

CASA NETWORK
BIBLESTUDYSERIES

GENERATIONS TOGETHER

PETER MENCONI

MT. SAGE PUBLISHING

Mt. Sage Publishing
Centennial, CO 80122

TABLE OF CONTENTS

ABOUT THE CASA NETWORK

In 1983, three Southern California churches established the CASA Network ministry to serve their 50+ members through cooperative efforts. The first jointly sponsored one day event was called Jamboree (now Life Celebration). The response to this first event led to a three day retreat held at a Christian conference center. A committee representing various churches met the next year to discover how to meet the growing needs of the Christian adult senior community and to discuss incorporating. They determined that the name of the new organization would be called CASA, Christian Association of Senior Adults.

In 1993 the CASA Board of Directors caught the vision to broaden its ministry to mid and post career age men and women nationally and internationally. In the fall of 1994, CASA launched two quarterly publications – The Energizer for senior adults and Energizing Leaders for leaders of Adults 50+ in the local church. With the explosion of the Boomer generation, a third quarterly publication was launched in 2001 for this population, called Legacy Living. For a time, CASA engaged in a website partnership with Christianity Today.

From 1993 through 1998 regional leadership training conferences were offered to pastors and lay leaders of adult 50+ ministries in a number of states and Canada. In 1998, the first National Leadership Training Conference was held in Irvine, CA and brought together over 300 pastors and lay leaders from 26 states and Canada. A further development in the growth of CASA's ministry was the establishment of a website **www.gocasa.org** that provides resources and information on 50+ ministry. Serving leaders across the country, the CASA Network offers regional, national, and international 50+ leadership conferences. You can access the CASA Network website at **www.gocasa.org** for the latest information on training offerings.

Today, the CASA Network is a premier training and equipping source for the Church's ministry to midlife and beyond age men and women. Augmented by internet and print media, the CASA Network brings together an array of leaders within the field of 50+ ministry to inspire and equip the Church for ministry to and through adults in life's second half. Only God knows how many lives have been touched, how many churches have been changed, how many leaders have been trained because of the vision and leadership of the CASA Network. Check us out at **www.gocasa.org** and welcome to the CASA Network Aging Well Bible Study Series.

BEFORE YOU BEGIN!
Instructions on how to get the most out of this book.

The primary purpose of this Bible study is to help you to take a fresh look at our current generations, how the generations relate, and how we can be better together.

This book contains six Bible study sessions on the topic of generations that can be done individually or in a small group. The studies are written for people who have never studied the Bible, occasionally study the Bible, or often study the Bible. That is, virtually everyone interested in intergenerational relationships will benefit from these studies. Each session allows the Bible to speak to where you are and where God may want you to go.

While these studies can be done individually, they are primarily designed to be done in a small group setting. In fact, you will receive maximum benefit when the study is discussed in a group. The more diverse your group is in age and experience, the more you will learn from these studies.

SUGGESTIONS ON FORMING A GROUP

1. Form a group that has between eight and 15 members. Groups larger or smaller are generally less effective.

2. One person should be appointed as the group facilitator. The facilitator's primary role is to get everyone together at an appointed time and place. The facilitator also gets the study started and keeps it going without getting off track. After the initial meeting the facilitator role can rotate within the group.

3. At the first meeting have the group members introduce themselves to one another and have each person share his or her responses to the following questions:

a) Where were you born and raised?

b) Where were you and what were you doing at age 10? Age 18? Age 25?

c) What one person, place, or experience has had the greatest impact on your life and why?

4. Before starting the study group members should agree on the length and frequency of meeting times. Normally, each study should take about one hour. All group members should commit themselves to attending all group sessions, unless there are circumstances beyond their control.

5. Give time for the small group to gel. Don't expect everything to click in the first session or two.

Because the interaction in a small group can reach into personal areas, it is important that group members agree upon "ground rules."

SUGGESTED GROUND RULES FOR SMALL GROUP STUDY

1. Jesus said that "the Holy Spirit, whom the Father will send in my name, will teach you all things and will remind you of everything I said to you." With this in mind, each group session should open in prayer asking the Holy Spirit to teach and guide. (Not everyone needs to pray. If a person is uncomfortable praying in public, he or she should be given freedom to remain silent.)

2. No one or two persons should dominate the discussion time. All group members should have an equal opportunity to express their thoughts, feelings, and experiences.

3. Because people's experiences and perspectives vary, there will be ideas, thoughts, and feelings expressed which will be quite diverse. All members should respect one another's perspective.

4. Confidentiality on what is said in the study should be agreed upon by all group members.

5. If significant conflict arises between specific group members, they should make every effort to resolve this conflict apart from group time. That is, they should agree to meet together at another time to discuss their differences.

6. If the group ends in prayer, members should pray for one another.

SESSION 1 | GENERATIONS TODAY

INTRODUCTION
Have one or more group members read the introduction aloud.

The Issue: What are the current generations, how do they differ, and how do they relate?

The new longevity, with people living longer, has created a generational phenomenon that is unique to modern times. Never before in recorded history have so many generations been alive at the same time. Today, there exists the possibility of 6 generations being alive in the same family. The current generations stretch from the GI Generation to Generation Z (yet to be "officially" named). These generations can span 100 years, so imagine the differences in worldviews and lifestyles that exist between the generations. Yet, most people are unaware of the ways that generational differences impact families, workplaces, schools, churches and other places where the different generations relate.

Think about your family. How different are the youngest family members from the oldest? Do any of your family members have tattoos or body piercings? How were these adornments received by older family members? How about music? Do younger and older members of your family share the same musical tastes? How radically do they differ? Does your extended family have members of other races? If so, how has this affected family dynamics? You get the point. The existence of multiple generations in our families has brought a greater range of life experiences and greater complexities.

Think about your workplace or church. How have they changed in the past 10 - 15 years? Does your workplace or church seem more chaotic today? Do you find yourself withdrawing at work because it takes too much effort to relate to younger people? Do you feel like your church has been hijacked by younger people and you hardly recognize it any more? These experiences are common among older adults because of generational differences.

If we are to stay in the game as we age, it is imperative that we understand the other generations. None of us, no matter what generation we are in, can overlook the fact that we are better together. But we will all need to work at it.

A brief overview of each of the generations will help raise your awareness of how and why we should pay attention to the differences and similarities in the generations. The following table will summarize important characteristics of 5 of the 6 current generations. (Generation Z is still in the formative stage.) These characteristics are generalizations that fit most, but not all, members of a generation.

	GI Generation 1906-24	Silent Generation 1925-43	Boomer Generation 1944-62	Generation X 1963-81	Millennial Generation 1982-2000
VALUES	God, Family, Country	Family, God, Security, Loyalty, Conformity	Competence, Consumerism, Excitement, Nonconformity, Relationships, Family	Self-reliance, Freedom, Skepticism, Fun and Humor, Friends, Family	Image, Money, Fame, Success, Causes, Technology, Friends/Family
WORK ETHIC	Work hard, Do whatever it takes, Work is a duty	Work hard, Expect to be rewarded, Work is an obligation	Workaholic, The one with the most toys wins, Work is an adventure	Work to live, Not live to work, Work is a necessary evil	Work should be fun and fast, Work should meet my needs
PLAY ETHIC	Work before play	Work until retirement, then play	Work hard, play hard	Play hard, Work only if necessary	Work and play all the time
MOTIVATORS	Sense of duty	Need for respect	Being valued and needed	Freedom for personal time	Flexibilty, Social networking
COMMUNICATION STYLE	Direct, Impersonal	Formal, Guarded	Informal, Face to face	Irreverent, Direct and short	Digitally, Constant

	Chain of command	Hierarchi-cal, Titles, Commit-tees	Informal, Networks of relation-ships	Everyone on their own, Just do your job and leave me alone	Non-hier-archical, Level play-ing field, Egalitarian
LEADER-SHIP STYLE					
TECHNOL-OGY	Radio, Black and white TV, Foreigners to technol-ogy	Transis-tor radio, Color TV, Immigrants to technol-ogy	Desktop com-puters, Walkmans, Mostly im-migrants to technol-ogy	Laptop comput-ers, iPods, Natives to technol-ogy	Tablets, Everything wireless, Restless natives to Technol-ogy

© 2013 Peter Menconi

As we read the Bible, we see that generations have always been important to God. In Genesis 17:7 we read "I will establish my cov-enant as an everlasting covenant between me and you and your descendants after you for the generations to come, to be your God and the God of your descendants after you." In this study we will see how God intended all the generations to be better together.

YOUR TAKE
Read and respond to the following questions. Discuss your responses with your group.

1. As you observe your friends, family members, coworkers, and oth-ers from different generations, which of the following statements best describes your attitude toward other generations?

__ People from other generations are just like me.

__ Younger generations are all messed up.

__ Older generations are out of touch.

__ If all the different generations would talk to each other, we all would learn something.

__ It isn't the generations that are different, it is the time of life that makes them different.

__ Human nature is the same in every generation.

___ I only relate and talk to people in my generation and ignore the others.

___ It is hopeless for the different generations to try to communicate.

___ Other _____.

2. As you look at the generational grid in the introduction, what generational differences surprise you the most?

YOUR REFLECTION

Read the following passages from the Bible and answer the questions that follow.

They are corrupt and not his children;
to their shame they are a warped and crooked generation.
Is this the way you repay the Lord,
you foolish and unwise people?
Is he not your Father, your Creator,
who made you and formed you?
Remember the days of old;
consider the generations long past.
Ask your father and he will tell you,
your elders, and they will explain to you.
—Deuteronomy 32:5-7

1. What might cause God to describe a generation as warped and crooked?

2. Why is it important for us to consider the generations that have come before us?

3. What is the responsibility (if any) of current generations to the ones that come after them?

All the ends of the earth will remember and turn to the Lord, and all the families of the nations will bow down before him, for dominion belongs to the Lord and he rules over the nations.

All the rich of the earth will feast and worship; all who go down to the dust will kneel before him—those who cannot keep themselves alive.

Posterity will serve him; future generations will be told about the Lord. They will proclaim his righteousness, declaring to a people yet unborn: He has done it!
—Psalm 22: 27-31

4. These verses are from a Messianic psalm that prophesizes the coming of Jesus Christ. What relationship does Jesus' coming have to the generations?

5. As followers of Jesus Christ, what responsibility do we have in making his coming to earth known to other generations?

YOUR APPLICATION

During the coming week, do the following exercises to help you better understand the different generations living today.

1. Go to a local mall or airport and do some people watching. What do you notice about the different generations you see? What do all the generations have in common? What is significantly different about the generations?

2. Talk to a friend, family member or coworker from a different generation. Ask them the following questions:

a. How do you view the similarities and differences between the generations?

b. Are you optimistic or pessimistic about the future?

c. How would you describe your worldview or the way you see life?

SESSION 2 | GENERATIONS IN THE CHURCH

INTRODUCTION
Have one or more group members read the introduction aloud.

The Issue: How well do different generations in the church understand each other and how well do they relate?

In the past several decades, most local churches have undergone a generational transformation. While it is still possible to have five, or even six, generations in a local church, more and more churches are segregating themselves according to age. In fact, many local churches are undergoing a slow death because members of Gen X and the Millennial Generation are no longer attending. By contrast, many so-called emerging churches have been started that cater primarily to the styles and needs of the younger generations.

In either case, churches whose attendees are of the same or similar generations are at risk. It is well documented that numerous mainline churches have aged, causing attendance to drop and churches to close. In addition, some churches with primarily Gen X and Millennial attendees are struggling because many younger people do not contribute financially well to ministry.

There are numerous reasons why the generations do not mix well in most local churches. Some of the major differences between the generations are triggered by values, music, dress, worship, work, and play styles. Often external appearances will keep older adults from relating to younger people, and vice versa. But many of the issues that keep the generations apart are about style and not substance. That is, many issues are superficial and need to be ignored.

If local churches are to be truly intergenerational, all generations will need to work at understanding each other better. The following table will help you to more fully understand the other generations in your church.

	GI Generation	Silent Generation	Boomer Generation	Generation X	Millennial Generation
WORSHIP STYLE	Formal/traditional	Traditional/predictable	Informal	Eclectic/artistic/informal	Eclectic/informal
WORSHIP MUSIC	Traditional hymns	Traditional hymns, choruses	Contemporary choruses	New emergent songs	Some of all types of music
PREACHING/TEACHING	Practical	Professional	Relational	Interactive	Integrated
COMMUNITY	Family-based	Collegial	Networks of relationships	Tribes	Global
LEADERSHIP STYLE	Chain of command	Corporate/committees	Team	Individualistic	"Three-dimensional"
THEOLOGY/FAITH	Private	Propositional	Practical	Contextual	Global
VIEW OF GOD	Distant father	Creator and truthgiver	Friend and ally	Compassionate healer	Global connector
WORLDVIEW	God is in control of the world	The laws of the universe are at work	The physical, emotional and spiritual worlds are all interrelated	The world is chaotic and broken	The world can be "fixed"
VALUES	Family/country/security	Truth/education/security	Tolerance/money/time	Genuineness/acceptance/fun	Competence/options
WORK ETHIC	"Do whatever it takes"	Loyalty/stable work/longevity	Work hard/play hard/meaningful work	Work to play/frequent job changes	Work as a "video game"/variety
RELATIONSHIP	More formal and positional	Congenial and sense of propriety	Informal and competitive	Individualistic and tribal	Friendships within groups
NEEDS	Acceptance/companionship	Inclusion/stability in midst of chaos	Sense of purpose and significance to "change the world"	Sense of belonging/hope/opportunities to "heal"/mentors	Intergenerational acceptance and understanding/mentors

Taken from *The Intergenerational Church: Understanding Congregations from WWII to www.com* by Peter Menconi

YOUR TAKE

Read and respond to the following questions. Discuss your responses with your group.

1. Which of the following statements best describe the ways the different generations in your church relate?

___ There is no tension between the different generations in our church.

___ The different generations in our church pass like ships in the night.

___ We have effective programs that bring the generations together.

___ We are struggling to become more intergenerational.

___ We don't even know we have an intergenerational problem.

___ Our church is multigenerational, but not intergenerational.

___ There is a lot of tension between the different generations in our church.

2. If your church became more intergenerational, how would you feel?

___ I would love to see the generations relate better.

___ I feel that it is futile to try to be more intergenerational.

___ I would like to do what I can to see the different generations relate better.

___ I feel that every generation has something to offer, so we should work at it.

___ I feel my generation would lose something if we became more intergenerational.

___ I feel that the older generations should decide how a church functions.

___ Other _____.

YOUR REFLECTION

Read the following passages from the Bible and answer the questions that follow.

Show me your ways, Lord, teach me your paths. Guide me in your truth and teach me, for you are God my Savior, and my hope is in you all day long. Remember, Lord, your great mercy and love, for they are from of old. Do not remember the sins of my youth and my rebellious ways; according to your love remember me, for you, LORD, are good.
—Psalm 25:4-7

1. As you think of your youth, were you rebellious or compliant? Explain your response, if you are comfortable.

2. Do you see today's youth as more or less rebellious than you were? Give an example or two that supports your response.

Light is sweet, and it pleases the eyes to see the sun. However many years anyone may live, let them enjoy them all. But let them remember the days of darkness, for there be many. Everything to come is meaningless.

You who are young, be happy while you are young, and let your heart give you joy in the days of your youth. Follow the ways of your heart and whatever your eyes see, but know that for all these things God will bring you into judgment.

So then, banish anxiety from your heart and cast off the troubles of your body, for youth and vigor are meaningless.
—Ecclesiastes 11:7-10

3. The writer of Ecclesiastes is searching for meaning in life. Do you identify with this search for meaning? If so, how has a search for meaning played out in your life?

4. Was your youth a happy or sad time? Please elaborate on your response.

5. Do you ever resent younger people because of their vigor and youth? Would you like to go back and relive the first half of you life? If so, why? If not, why not?

6. What lessons in life have you learned that you feel you can pass on to younger people?

YOUR APPLICATION

During the coming weeks, do the following exercises to help you better understand the different generations in your church.

1. The next time you are in church, stand in the narthex or foyer and assess the generational makeup of your church. Are all generations present or is your church made up primarily of one or two generations?

2. Begin to think about how your church can become more multi and intergenerational. Discuss your concerns with other church members and, if possible, church leaders.

3. Begin to be more intentional about relating to people in your church who are of a different generation. Go to coffee or lunch with younger people, or have them over for dinner, or consider becoming a mentor to them.

SESSION 3 | GENERATIONAL TENSION

INTRODUCTION
Have one or more group members read the introduction aloud.

The Issue: How are you dealing with the intergenerational tension in your family, workplace, church or elsewhere?

Major differences between our current generations can produce ongoing conflict and tension. Intergenerational conflict is present in most families, among friends, between coworkers, in most churches, and virtually everywhere the different generations interact. Older generations often see younger people as rude, crude, and disrespectful. Younger generations can see older adults as out of touch, a burden on society, and generally in their way.

In our families and homes generational differences in values and worldviews often lead to intense arguments and alienations. Styles of dress, tattoos, sexual behavior, work ethics, and other behaviors among younger members of a family can be a constant irritant to parents, grandparents, and even older siblings. Younger people may be annoyed as they see their parents as unaware and old-fashioned. Further tension may result when boomerang kids return to living at home when emerging adulthood becomes too difficult.

Tensions between parents and their kids often do not subside even after children are grown. Many older adults find themselves in conflict with adult children just when they thought their parenting days were over. There can be numerous issues that create tension: lifestyle choices, finances, divorce, childrearing, career choices, work ethic, religion, politics, and more. Often issues from childhood and adolescence can surface when children become adults. Mother-adult daughter tension can be especially intense. In addition, adult children may have mixed emotions about providing care giving for their aging parents.

The workplace is another environment where intergenerational tension can exist. With four or more generations in a workplace, some conflict is inevitable. While many members of a generation do not fit stereotypes, there are certain characteristics that are fairly consistent within generations. Older workers, especially from the Silent Generation, have a strong work ethic with a "just get it done" attitude. Boomers are often seen as workaholics who value teamwork, hierarchical leadership, and face to face communication. By contrast, Gen Xers are independent and self-reliant and do not want to spend more time at work than necessary. They value their personal time and are not patient with trivia and small talk. The new entrants into the workforce, the Millennials, are ambitious and tech-savvy. They would rather communicate through technology and are impatient with working in an office where life doesn't move fast enough.

Many of these same generational characteristics are brought into our churches. The Silents usually prefer traditional worship with hymns and a choir. They often see the pastor as a qualified profes-sional whose job is to teach them how to be Christians. Boomers were the generation that brought guitars, drums, and keyboards to worship services. They value participation and prefer choruses that get the congregation singing. The use of drama, poetry, videos, and informal sermons were also introduced by Boomers. Gen Xers were the first generation to exit our churches in large numbers. If they were interested in gathering for worship, they often started their own generational churches, giving rise to the Emergent Church movement. Millennials may attend church with their parents until they leave high school. If they have spiritual interests at all, it is of-ten satisfied through technology and interaction with their friends.

While the generational differences in our homes, workplaces, churches, and elsewhere can create tension, it is imperative that older adults take the lead in minimizing these tensions. If we are to see greater intergenerational harmony, it will take flexibility and openness from older adults toward younger people. It is worth the effort because the different generations are better together.

YOUR TAKE

Read and respond to the following questions. Discuss your responses with your group.

1. Which of the following issues produce tension between you and younger adults in your life?

__ Jobs

__ Education

__ Finances

__ Housekeeping

__ Lifestyle

__ Health

__ Communication

__ Intrusion into adult children's lives

__ Unsolicited advice

__ Marriage and dating

__ Having children

__ Child-rearing practices

__ Politics

__ Religion

__ Sexual behavior

__ Criticism

__ Personal demands

__ Lack of boundaries

__ Other _____.

2. Do you currently have tension and conflict between yourself and someone of another generation? What is this tension and how might you resolve it?

YOUR REFLECTION

Read the following passages from the Bible and answer the questions that follow.

Now a man of God came to Eli and said to him, "This is what the Lord says: 'Did I not clearly reveal myself to your ancestor's family when they were in Egypt under Pharaoh? I chose your ancestor out of all the tribes of Israel to be my priest, to go up to my altar, to burn incense, and to wear an ephod in my presence. I also gave your ancestor's family all the food offerings presented by the Israelites. Why do you scorn my sacrifice and offering that I prescribed for my dwelling? Why do you honor your sons more than me by fattening yourselves on the choice parts of every offering made by my people Israel?'

"Therefore the Lord, the God of Israel, declares: 'I promised that members of your family would minister before me forever.' But now the Lord declares: 'Far be it from me! Those who honor me I will honor, but those who despise me will be disdained. The time is coming when I will cut short your strength and the strength of your priestly house, so that no one in it will reach old age, and you will see distress in my dwelling. Although good will be done to Israel, no one in your family line will ever reach old age. Every one of you that I do not cut off from serving at my altar I will spare only to destroy your sight and sap your strength, and all your descendants will die in the prime of life.

And what happens to your two sons, Hophni and Phinehas, will be a sign to you—they will both die on the same day. I will raise up for myself a faithful priest, who will do according to what is in my heart and mind. I will firmly establish his priestly house, and they will minister before my anointed one always. Then everyone left in your family line will come and bow down before him for a piece of silver and a loaf of bread and plead, "Appoint me to some priestly office so I can have food to eat."'
—1 Samuel 2:27-36

1. Eli was the high priest of Israel who had two disobedient sons, Hophni and Phinehas (also priests). From these verses, how well did Eli parent his sons?

2. Eli did not confront the bad behavior of his sons. What is God's response to the disobedience of both Eli and his sons? Does this story have anything to say to us about confronting conflict between the generations? If so, what?

Some time later Paul said to Barnabas, "Let us go back and visit the believers in all the towns where we preached the word of the Lord and see how they are doing." Barnabas wanted to take John, also called Mark, with them, but Paul did not think it wise to take him, because he had deserted them in Pamphylia and had not continued with them in the work. They had such a sharp disagreement that they parted company. Barnabas took Mark and sailed for Cyprus, but Paul chose Silas and left, commended by the believers to the grace of the Lord. He went through Syria and Cilicia, strengthening the churches.
—Acts 15: 36-41

3. A dispute arises between the apostle Paul and Barnabas over John Mark. (John Mark was Barnabas' nephew). Why didn't Paul want to take John Mark on their journey? How might Paul's position be similar to the ways we view younger people?

4. Who was right in this dispute? Would you have reacted more like Paul or more like Barnabas? Why?

From that time on Jesus began to explain to his disciples that he must go to Jerusalem and suffer many things at the hands of the elders, the chief priests and the teachers of the law, and that he must be killed and on the third day be raised to life.

Peter took him aside and began to rebuke him. "Never, Lord!" he said. "This shall never happen to you!" Jesus turned and said to Peter, "Get behind me, Satan! You are a stumbling block to me; you do not have in mind the concerns of God, but merely human concerns."
—Matthew 16:21-23

5. While Peter was probably Jesus' oldest disciple, he was still younger than Jesus. (It is estimated that the average life span during Jesus' time was about 24 years old). Why did Jesus rebuke Peter?

6. In what ways are intergenerational tensions and conflicts more about human concerns than spiritual concerns?

YOUR APPLICATION

During the coming weeks, do the following exercises to help you better understand the intergenerational tension and conflict that might exist in your life.

1. Find a quiet place and take 15 minutes or so to think about your intergenerational relationships. Write done any issues you may have with people of other generations. Pray about these areas of tension and conflict and ask for guidance on how to resolve them.

2. After prayer and reflection, take action to resolve these intergenerational issues. Be gracious and wise. If necessary, seek the advice of someone you respect before taking action. Don't overlook getting advice from a younger person.

SESSION 4 | INTERGENERATIONAL RELATIONSHIPS

INTRODUCTION
Have one or more group members read the introduction aloud.

The Issue: How can you develop healthy relationships with other generations that are mutually edifying?

Intergenerational relationships do not have to be tense or in conflict. In fact, today more than ever, we need the different generations talking to each other. Life has changed significantly for both younger and older people and many of us have lost our way. Healthy intergenerational relationships afford all generations the opportunity to learn from each other. If we relate primarily to people in our generation, we miss the chance to give and receive wisdom that will better our journey through life.

Today older adults have an excellent opportunity to develop healthy relationship with younger people. And contrary to popular opinion, most young people would like to have relationships with older adults who they can trust. For example, many grandparents know that they have special relationships with their grandchildren, even when they become adults.

Unfortunately, most young people will not initiate a relationship with an older adult, even when they need help or would like some guidance. If an intergenerational relationship is to be established, it is usually the responsibility of an older adult to start it. Initiating an intergenerational relationship can be formal or informal. That is, it can be done through a structured mentoring program or as an outgrowth of a relationship that already exists.

Followers of Jesus Christ should be especially motivated to invest in younger generations. Like the psalmist, we should pray, "Even when I am old and gray, do not forsake me, my God, till I declare your power to the next generation, your mighty acts to all who are to come."

Even with the best of intentions, older adults may find an intergenerational relationship difficult to navigate. Generational differences are real and can often lead to misunderstandings in communication. Even when a relationship is based on mutual respect and concern, the older adult may need to exercise an extra measure of grace. But despite the potential difficulties, intergenerational relationships are well worth the effort. In fact, if older adults do not step up to invest in younger people, our culture and society will be the poorer.

So, get out of your comfort zone and develop an intergenerational relationship that will enrich your life and be a blessing to a younger person.

YOUR TAKE

Read and respond to the following questions. Discuss your responses with your group.

1. How do you feel about establishing intergenerational relationships?

___ I am already a mentor to a younger person.

___ I had to find my own way in life; younger people need to do the same.

___ I think many young people have lost their way and need our help.

___ I would like to help younger people, but I'm not sure if I have anything to offer.

___ I would like to have an intergenerational relationship, but I'm scared.

___ I feel that I would make a good mentor or coach.

___ I feel like it would be too much work.

___ I am open to the idea, but don't know where to start.

___ I feel like most young people wouldn't listen to me.

___ I don't think I have the patience for younger people.

___ Other _____.

2. Are you currently aware of any healthy intergenerational relationships in your family, workplace, church or elsewhere? If so, share your observations with your group.

YOUR REFLECTION

Read the following passages from the Bible and answer the questions that follow.

Note: The following passage and conversation occurred after both of Naomi's sons died. One of the sons was Ruth's husband (making Naomi her mother-in-law).

But Naomi said, "Return home, my daughters. Why would you come with me? Am I going to have any more sons, who could become your husbands? Return home, my daughters; I am too old to have another husband. Even if I thought there was still hope for me—even if I had a husband tonight and then gave birth to sons—would you wait until they grew up? Would you remain unmarried for them? No, my daughters. It is more bitter for me than for you, because the Lord's hand has turned against me!"

At this they wept aloud again. Then Orpah kissed her mother-in-law goodbye, but Ruth clung to her. "Look," said Naomi, "your sister-in-law is going back to her people and her gods. Go back with her."

But Ruth replied, "Don't urge me to leave you or to turn back from you. Where you go I will go, and where you stay I will stay. Your people will be my people and your God my God. Where you die I will die, and there I will be buried. May the Lord deal with me, be it ever so severely,

if even death separates you and me." When Naomi realized that Ruth was determined to go with her, she stopped urging her.
—Ruth 1: 11-18

1. How was this intergenerational relationship established between Naomi and Ruth? Was it planned or did it develop as a natural occurrence as they lived life?

2. Is this intergenerational relationship one-sided? What might each woman be getting and/or giving in this relationship?

In the presence of God and of Christ Jesus, who will judge the living and the dead, and in view of his appearing and his kingdom, I give you this charge: Preach the word; be prepared in season and out of season; correct, rebuke and encourage—with great patience and careful instruction.

For the time will come when people will not put up with sound doctrine. Instead, to suit their own desires, they will gather around them a great number of teachers to say what their itching ears want to hear. They will turn their ears away from the truth and turn aside to myths. But you, keep your head in all situations, endure hardship, do the work of an evangelist, discharge all the duties of your ministry.

For I am already being poured out like a drink offering, and the time for my departure is near. I have fought the good fight, I have finished the race, I have kept the faith. Now there is in store for me the crown of

righteousness, which the Lord, the righteous Judge, will award to me on that day—and not only to me, but also to all who have longed for his appearing.
—2 Timothy 4:1-8

3. The apostle Paul was Timothy's mentor. In this letter to Timothy, what roles of a mentor do you see Paul fulfilling?

4. Paul took Timothy along on his missionary journeys. How does spending time together strengthen an intergenerational relationship?

5. Paul is getting near the end of his life. In what ways do you think aging affects a mentoring relationship?

6. In what ways do you think Timothy benefited from this relationship?

YOUR APPLICATION

During the coming weeks, do the following exercises to help you move toward the establishment of healthy intergenerational relationships.

1. Spend some time thinking about the intergenerational relationships in your life. In what ways can these relationships change to make them more mutually beneficial?

2. Think about younger people who you can possibly mentor. Consider individual, couples or group mentoring. Go to the internet or your local library to educate yourself on mentoring. There are many resources available on how to be a good mentor. Step out of your comfort zone to establish some healthy intergenerational relationships.

SESSION 5 | INTERGENERATIONAL MINISTRY

INTRODUCTION
Have one or more group members read the introduction aloud.

The Issue: How can older adults minister more effectively to younger generations?

In the past decade or two numerous articles and books have been written on why so many young adults leave our churches. Studies by the Barna Group uncovered six significant themes why nearly three out of every five young Christians after age 15 disconnect, either permanently or for an extended period of time, from church life:

Reason #1 – Churches seem overprotective.

Reason #2 – Teens' and twentysomethings' experience of Christianity is shallow.

Reason #3 – Churches come across as antagonistic to science.

Reason #4 – Young Christians' church experiences related to sexuality are often simplistic, judgmental.

Reason #5 – They wrestle with the exclusive nature of Christianity.

Reason #6 – The church feels unfriendly to those who doubt.

There is a very significant gap between the ways older adults view the world and spirituality and the ways the younger generations do. If you are not sure this gap exists, sit down with some young people to hear their views on life. You will see that the secularization of American society has happened quite rapidly. It isn't that young people are not concerned about spirituality, they are. But they are making it up as they go along.

In their book *Soul Searching: The Religious and Spiritual Lives of American Teenagers*, sociologists Christian Smith and Melinda Lundquist Denton summarize the conclusions from over 3000 interviews with teenagers. From these interviews they coined a term that describes the common religious beliefs of American youth; they call it Moralistic Therapeutic Deism. The combination of beliefs of Moralistic Therapeutic Deism are that:

1. A god exists who created and ordered the world and watches over human life on earth.

2. God wants people to be good, nice, and fair to each other, as taught in the Bible and by most world religions.

3. The central goal of life is to be happy and to feel good about oneself.

4. God does not need to be particularly involved in one's life except when God is needed to resolve a problem.

5. Good people go to heaven when they die.

Needless to say, MTD does not line up well with the orthodox Christian teachings of the Bible. It is also apparent that older generations of Christ followers will need to educate themselves on the spiritual views of younger generations before a conversational connect can take place. If serious Christians of older generations are to have an influence on younger generations, it is imperative that these conversations take place. Not only can and must the gospel be spoken by older believers, it must also be modeled.

Want help? In his book *You Lost Me: Why Young Christians Are Leaving Church*, David Kinnaman solicits 50 ideas from other Christian leaders to help older and younger adults reconnect with each other and the gospel. Examples of their suggestions are: be honest, confess, preach a better gospel, invite participation, re-center on Jesus, be intentionally intergenerational, disciple like Jesus, and many more helpful ideas.

Today, older adults have a wonderful opportunity to influence and guide the younger generations. God has always called his older children to take spiritual responsibility for the younger generations. It will not be easy and will take some proactive intentionality. But the personal and corporate results will be well worth it. Now is the time for concerned, compassionate Christ followers to start an intergenerational ministry movement that will transform the worldwide church.

YOUR TAKE

Read and respond to the following questions. Discuss your responses with your group.

1. The following are criticisms many young people have about the church. Which do you think are valid and which do you think are invalid? Discuss your responses with your group.

___ Churches seem overprotective.

___ Their experience of Christianity in the church is shallow.

___ Churches come across as antagonistic to science.

___ The church's approach to sexuality is often simplistic and judgmental.

___ The church sees Christianity as unique, exclusive, and different than other religions.

___ The church feels unfriendly to those who doubt.

2. If older adults are to minister to younger people, which of the following perspectives and actions will need to be initiated?

___ Learn to appreciate differences

___ Center conversations on Jesus

___ Tell others what to do

___ Educate yourself on different generations

___ Admit not knowing everything

___ Proactively build relationships

___ Learn to serve

___ Stretch your comfort zone

___ Don't condescend

___ Straighten out the prodigal

___ Share lessons learned the hard way

___ Protect young people from life's realities

___ Learn to actively listen

___ Don't overreact

__ Pay attention to cultural trends

__ Help strengthen families

__ Communicate humbly

__ Pull rank when necessary

__ Develop young leaders

__ Tell your story

__ Be a wise mentor

__ Talk clearly

__ Think clearly

__ Encourage realistically

YOUR REFLECTION

Read the following passages from the Bible and answer the questions that follow.

My people, hear my teaching; listen to the words of my mouth. I will open my mouth with a parable; I will utter hidden things, things from of old— things we have heard and known, things our ancestors have told us.

We will not hide them from their descendants; we will tell the next generation the praiseworthy deeds of the LORD, his power, and the wonders he has done.

He decreed statutes for Jacob and established the law in Israel, which he commanded our ancestors to teach their children, so the next generation would know them, even the children yet to be born, and they in turn would tell their children.

Then they would put their trust in God and would not forget his deeds but would keep his commands.
They would not be like their ancestors—a stubborn and rebellious generation,whose hearts were not loyal to God, whose spirits were not faithful to him.
—Psalm 78: 1-8

1. What are the responsibilities of the older generations toward the younger generations?

2. If these responsibilities are done well by the older generations, what results? How are these verses relevant to us today?

Paul, an apostle of Christ Jesus by the will of God, in keeping with the promise of life that is in Christ Jesus,

To Timothy, my dear son:

Grace, mercy and peace from God the Father and Christ Jesus our Lord.

I thank God, whom I serve, as my ancestors did, with a clear conscience, as night and day I constantly remember you in my prayers. Recalling your tears, I long to see you, so that I may be filled with joy. I am reminded of your sincere faith, which first lived in your grandmother Lois and in your mother Eunice and, I am persuaded, now lives in you also.

For this reason I remind you to fan into flame the gift of God, which is in you through the laying on of my hands. For the Spirit God gave us does not make us timid, but gives us power, love and self-discipline. So do not be ashamed of the testimony about our Lord or of me his prisoner. Rather, join with me in suffering for the gospel, by the power of God. He has saved us and called us to a holy life—not because of anything we have done but because of his own purpose and grace. This grace was given us in Christ Jesus before the beginning of time.
—2 Timothy 1:1-9

3. In this letter, how would you describe Paul's attitude toward Timothy?

4. What is the significance and importance of Paul mentioning Timothy's mother and grandmother?

5. What does it mean to "fan into flame" the gift that God has put in the heart of another person? How would you fan into flame the gifts and abilities God has put in the heart of a young person?

6. If we are not to be timid for Jesus Christ, how should we act?

YOUR APPLICATION

During the coming week, do the following exercises to help you move toward the establishment of healthy intergenerational ministry.

1. Take some time alone to reflect on the following questions: Did you have a mentor or mentors in your life? Who were they? What did they do to mentor you? How has their influence in your life changed you? What have you learned that you can pass on to younger people?

2. As you think about the possibilities of ministering across the generations, what are your hopes and fears? What would motive you to reach out and minister to a younger person? Is there a current relationship or two that can become a mentoring relationship? Think proactively on how you can become a ministering mentor.

SESSION 6 | BETTER TOGETHER

INTRODUCTION
Have one or more group members read the introduction aloud.

The Issue: We are all better when the different generations relate in a healthy way. How do we do this?

To this point in our study we have come to realize that intergenerational relationships are important. But, ideally, these relationships should be experienced in community and not in isolation. While there is much talk about community among Christians, there is relatively little being experienced. The church was meant to be an intergenerational community. From the very beginning of scripture we see the various generations represented and acknowledged. But along the way the church became more and more segregated according to age. Today, many local churches have age-based ministries that keep the different generations apart from each other. Most churches are multigenerational, but not intergenerational. A truly intergenerational church and experience intentionally involves all the generations in the life and activities of the community.

From scripture we can glean some important characteristics of a vital Christian community. First, a commitment to following Jesus Christ is central to the vitality and strength of a body of believers. Second, the regular practices of teaching and learning, corporate prayer, taking meals together, and fellowship underscore that our journey with Jesus is not solitary. Third, our first century brothers and sisters were generous in meeting practical needs within the church, such as providing food and finances. We are to do the same. There are other lessons and characteristics that can be lifted from the Bible and they can provide guidance in the establishment of an intergenerational community.

A factor in young people leaving churches is the failure to develop healthy relationships between the different generations. This trend needs to be reversed. It will take the proactive leading of older generations to initiate necessary changes. Here are some suggested steps that can be taken:

- Challenge the stereotypes of all the generations.
- Treat everyone in every generation with dignity; God does.
- Find common ground for meaningful conversations.
- Listen to each other with open minds.
- Appreciate and encourage the unique giftedness God has given to each of us.
- Passionately seek the unity Jesus Christ has called us to.
- Allow people of all generations to contribute and lead.
- Expect all generations to learn from each other.

Before he left this earth, Jesus Christ called his disciples and us to unity. In John 17: 20-23, Jesus prayed for all believers. "My prayer is not for them alone. I pray also for those who will believe in me through their message, that all of them may be one, Father, just as you are in me and I am in you. May they also be in us so that the world may believe that you have sent me. I have given them the glory that you gave me, that they may be one as we are one—I in them and you in me—so that they may be brought to complete unity. Then the world will know that you sent me and have loved them even as you have loved me."

For a local church to truly experience intergenerational community, each generation must honor and love one another above themselves. Tolerance of one another will not get it done. All members of the church must learn to genuinely appreciate people in the body who are different than themselves. Simply put, as brothers and sisters in God's family, we are on this journey together.

All of us, from every generation who are God's children, have been given his mission. God's mission is to redeem his broken creation. That is why the Father sent the Son; and the Father and the Son has sent the Spirit; and the Father, Son, and Spirit send us, the church, into the world to carry on his mission of redemption. The work of redemption has no age requirement. We are to be about God's work together; and we can do it better together.

YOUR TAKE

Read and respond to the following questions. Discuss your responses with your group.

1. Which of the following definitions best describes your understanding of community?

___ unified body of individuals

___ people with common interests living in a particular area

___ an interacting population of various kinds of individuals in a common location

___ a group of people with a common characteristic or interest living together within a larger society

___ a group linked by a common policy

___ a body of persons or nations having a common history or common social, economic, and political interests

___ a body of persons of common and especially professional interests scattered through a larger society

___ a social group of any size whose members reside in a specific locality, share government, and often have a common cultural and historical heritage

___ a social, religious, occupational, or other group sharing common characteristics or interests and perceived or perceiving itself as distinct in some respect from the larger society within which it exists

___ a group of men or women leading a common life according to shared beliefs

2. As you look back over your life experiences, can you think of a time or two when several generations came together to create something special? (For example, a short-term mission trip was a more moving experience because multiple generations were involved.)

YOUR REFLECTION
Read the following passages from the Bible and answer the questions that follow.

There are different kinds of gifts, but the same Spirit distributes them. There are different kinds of service, but the same Lord. There are different kinds of working, but in all of them and in everyone it is the same God at work.

Now to each one the manifestation of the Spirit is given for the common good. To one there is given through the Spirit a message of wisdom, to another a message of knowledge by means of the same Spirit, to another faith by the same Spirit, to another gifts of healing by that one Spirit, to another miraculous powers, to another prophecy, to another distinguishing between spirits, to another speaking in different kinds of tongues, and to still another the interpretation of tongues. All these are the work of one and the same Spirit, and he distributes them to each one, just as he determines.

Just as a body, though one, has many parts, but all its many parts form one body, so it is with Christ. For we were all baptized by one Spirit so as to form one body—whether Jews or Gentiles, slave or free—and we were all given the one Spirit to drink.
—1 Corinthians 12: 4-13

1. Christians are given different gifts to use in furthering God's kingdom. Do you know your spiritual gift or gifts? How are you using your gift or gifts?

2. In what tangible ways can the church, the body of Christ, experience unity in the face of diversity? In what ways have you experienced unity coming out of diversity?

3. In what ways can the different generations in the body come together to create unity?

Those who accepted his message were baptized, and about three thousand were added to their number that day. They devoted themselves to the apostles' teaching and to the fellowship, to the breaking of bread and to prayer. Everyone was filled with awe, and many wonders and miraculous signs were done by the apostles.

All the believers were together and had everything in common. Selling their possessions and goods, they gave to anyone as he had need. Every day they continued to meet together in the temple courts. They broke bread in their homes and ate together with glad and sincere hearts, praising God and enjoying the favor of all the people. And the Lord added to their number daily those who were being saved.
—Acts 2:41-47

4. What activities of the early church give us hints on how the Christian community should behave?

5. Every generation brings something to the table. How can intergenerational relationships and ministry make the church more effective in its witness for Jesus Christ?

YOUR APPLICATION

During the coming weeks reflect on the following suggestions and ideas, preferably with your group. Then start to act to help the different generations to be better together.

We can help to build an intergenerational community in numerous ways. As in other areas of the Christian life, creativity and innovation are quite helpful. The following suggestions on moving toward intergenerational community may be helpful, but each of us will need to customize our approach to fit our unique situation and culture. Here are some suggestions on how people in local churches can develop intergenerational community:

- Integrate multiple generations into the worship service as often as possible.
- Schedule regular multigenerational church events as a way of building intergenerational community.
- Schedule regular sporting events that engage multiple generations.
- Encourage family members to eat at least one meal a day together.
- Take opportunities to include non-nuclear family members in your family activities.
- Churches can create "new households" within the church community by encouraging non-nuclear families to meet and relate regularly. =
- There are more than 7 million grandparents in the United States who are daily helping to raise their grandchildren. Churches can help to provide support and community for grandparents in these situations.
- Churches can develop opportunities for multiple generations to tell stories about their lives and journeys of faith that can be shared during worship services, in classes, during mentoring times, or at intergenerational social events.
- Develop mentoring relationships between younger and older congregation members.
- Develop opportunities for people of various generations to share their interests and hobbies.

- Create opportunities for multiple generations to see movies or read specific books together.
- Establish opportunities for youth and young adults to be exposed to older members' workplaces.
- Organize regular intergenerational mission trips and outreach projects.
- Above all, be creative and plan intergenerational activities that fit your church's culture.

Now is the time for followers of Jesus Christ to begin an intergenerational movement in our churches and society. Older adults can take the lead and call younger people to lead with them. Bringing Jesus Christ to all generations is our call...let's get on with it!

FURTHER READING

Lost in Transition: The Dark Side of Emerging Adulthood by Christian Smith

The Intergenerational Church: Understanding Congregations from WWII to www.com by Peter Menconi

You Lost Me.: Why Young Christians are Leaving Church... by David Kinnaman

Shaping the Journey of Emerging Adults by Richard R. Dunn and Jana L. Sundene

The Next Wave: Empowering the Generation that Will Change Our World by David Wraight

Wisdom Meets Passion: When Generations Collide and Collaborate by Dan Miller and Jared Angaza

ABOUT THE AUTHOR

Peter Menconi has written and presented widely on generational and aging issues. His rich background as a dentist, pastor, counselor, business owner, conference speaker, husband, father, and grandfather brings unique perspectives to his writing.

Born and raised in Chicago, Pete graduated from the University of Illinois, College of Dentistry and practiced dentistry for 23 years in private practice, in the U.S. Army and in a mission hospital in Kenya, East Africa. In addition, Pete has a M.S. in Counseling Psychology and several years of seminary training. He has also been a commodity futures floor trader, a speaker with the American Dental Association, and a broker of medical and dental practices.

For over 20 years Pete was the outreach pastor at a large church in suburban Denver, Colorado. Currently, he is the president of Mt. Sage Publishing and board member with the CASA Network.

Pete's writings include the book *The Intergenerational Church: Understanding Congregations from WWII to www.com*, The Support Group Series, a 9-book Bible study series, and numerous articles.

Pete and his wife Jean live in the Denver area and they are the parents of 3 adult children and the grandparents of 9 grandchildren.

Pete Menconi can be reached at petermenconi@msn.com.

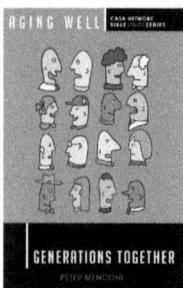

SAGE OR CURMUDGEON

The primary purpose of this Bible study is to help you to take a closer look at your attitude about aging, how to reevaluate your attitude, and how to move toward becoming a sage for younger people.

THE AGING FAMILY AND MARRIAGE

The primary purpose of this Bible study is to help you to take a closer look at your aging marriage and/or family and see how you can maximize these relationships.

FINISHING WELL

The primary purpose of this Bible study is to help you to take a closer look at how you can finish well before your life is over.

THE INTERGENERATIONAL CHURCH:
Understanding Congregations from WWII to www.com

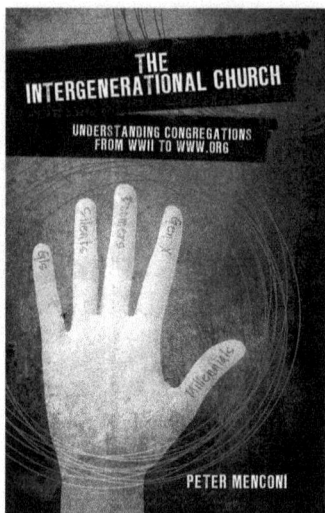

Are certain generations underrepresented in your church?

Would you like to see more young adults in your congregation?

The Intergenerational Church: Understanding Congregations from WWII to www.com will show you why understanding today's generations is crucial for the survival and thrival of the local church.

The Intergenerational Church is a breakthrough book that will help you meet the Intergenerational Challenge.

FROM THIS IMPORTANT BOOK, YOU WILL LEARN HOW TO:

- Minimize generational tension.
- Get all the generations moving in the same direction.
- Develop leaders from all generations.
- Deliver intergenerational preaching.
- Cultivate intergenerational worship and community.
- Stimulate intergenerational mission and outreach.

www.ingramcontent.com/pod-product-compliance
Lightning Source LLC
Chambersburg PA
CBHW051045030426
42339CB00006B/211